>YOU+DO-THE÷MATHS

Taking your maths skills to new heights!

DESIGN A
SKYSCRAPER

HILARY KOLL AND **STEVE MILLS**

ILLUSTRATED BY **VLADIMIR ALEKSIC**

QED

D1352918

Created for QED Publishing, Inc. by Tall Tree Ltd
Editor: Jon Richards
Designers: Ed Simkins and Jonathan Vipond

QED Editorial Director: Victoria Garrard
QED Art Director: Laura Roberts-Jensen
QED Editor: Tasha Percy
QED Designer: Krina Patel

First published in the UK in 2014 by
QED Publishing
A Quarto Group company
The Old Brewery
6 Blundell Street
London, N7 9BH

www.qed-publishing.co.uk

A catalogue record for this book is available
from the British Library.

ISBN 978 1 78171 693 9

Printed in China

CONTENTS

Hi, my name is Alice and I'm an architect. I'm going to show you how maths can help you build one of the biggest skyscrapers in the world!

SHAPES OF SKYSCRAPERS

You have been asked to design a towering skyscraper using the latest designs and cutting-edge technology and materials.

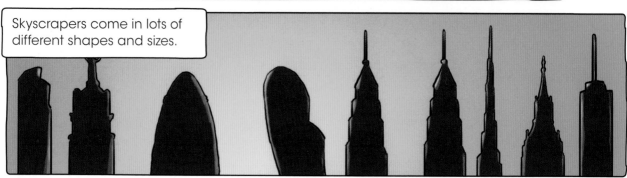

Skyscrapers come in lots of different shapes and sizes.

These shapes include cylinders, cuboids, **prisms**, **pyramids** and cones, or a combination of these.

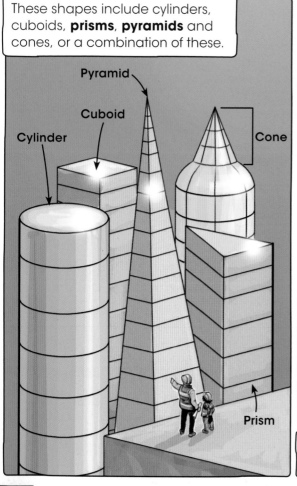

Pyramid

Cuboid

Cylinder

Cone

Prism

The Gherkin, London, UK

The ADNEC, Abu Dhabi, UAE

Modern skyscrapers also come in unusual curved shapes, like the two shown here.

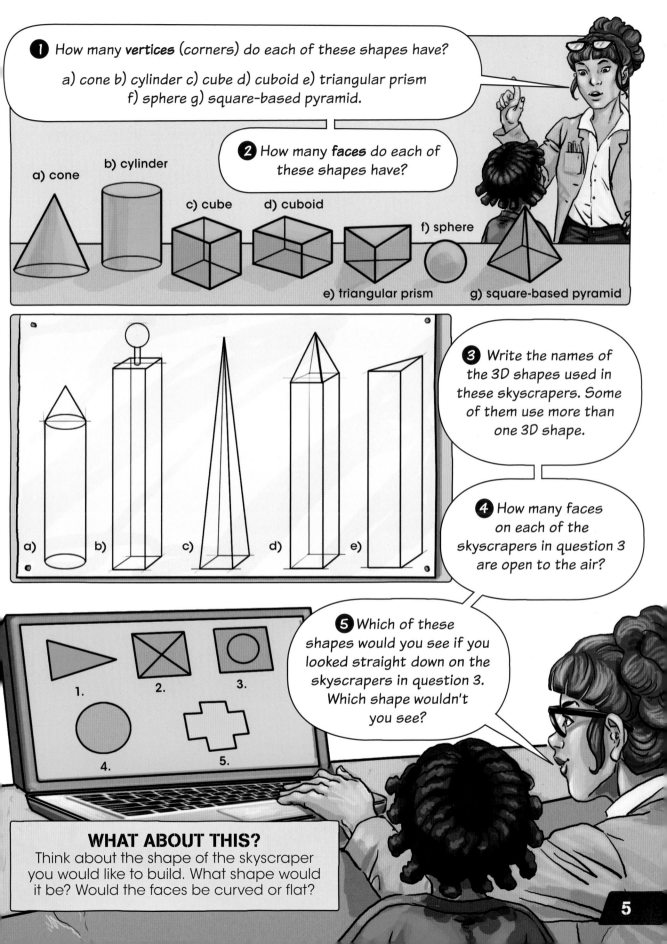

1 How many **vertices** (corners) do each of these shapes have?

a) cone b) cylinder c) cube d) cuboid e) triangular prism
f) sphere g) square-based pyramid.

2 How many **faces** do each of these shapes have?

a) cone
b) cylinder
c) cube
d) cuboid
e) triangular prism
f) sphere
g) square-based pyramid

3 Write the names of the 3D shapes used in these skyscrapers. Some of them use more than one 3D shape.

a) b) c) d) e)

4 How many faces on each of the skyscrapers in question 3 are open to the air?

5 Which of these shapes would you see if you looked straight down on the skyscrapers in question 3. Which shape wouldn't you see?

1. 2. 3. 4. 5.

WHAT ABOUT THIS?
Think about the shape of the skyscraper you would like to build. What shape would it be? Would the faces be curved or flat?

5

THE SIZE OF SKYSCRAPERS

New skyscrapers are being built all the time with the aim of being the tallest in the world. When one becomes the tallest, an even taller one is planned!

You have been asked to make your skyscraper one of the tallest in the world. You are looking at other tall buildings around the globe to see how yours will compare.

Makkah Royal Clock Tower, Saudi Arabia: 601 m

One World Trade Center, USA: 541 m

Big Ben, UK: 96 m

Empire State Building, USA: 381 m

Shanghai Tower, China: 632 m

Petronas Twin Towers, Malaysia: 452 m

Burj Khalifa, UAE: 828 m

This table shows the heights of some famous buildings, including some of the tallest towers on the planet.

NAME	COUNTRY	HEIGHT
Big Ben	UK	96 m
The Shard	UK	310 m
The Gherkin	UK	180 m
Empire State Building	USA	381 m
One World Trade Center	USA	541 m
Petronas Twin Towers	Malaysia	452 m
Taipei 101 Tower	Taiwan	509 m
Jin Mao Building	China	421 m
Burj Khalifa	UAE	828 m
Shanghai Tower	China	632 m
Makkah Royal Clock Tower	Saudi Arabia	601 m

1 How much taller is:

a) the Shard than the Gherkin?
b) the Jin Mao Building than the Empire State Building?
c) Burj Khalifa than Big Ben?

2 List the buildings in order of height from shortest to tallest.

Empire State Building, USA: 381 m

3 Which building is:

a) 31 metres taller than the Makkah Royal Clock Tower?
b) 120 metres taller than the Jin Mao Building?
c) 199 metres shorter than the Taipei 101 Tower?

4 Round the height of each building to the nearest 100 metres.

WHAT ABOUT THIS?
Find out the heights of the tallest buildings in the world before 1880 and create a table listing them in height order.

RECORD-BREAKING SKYSCRAPERS

As part of your research into other tall buildings, you have been looking into the history of skyscrapers.

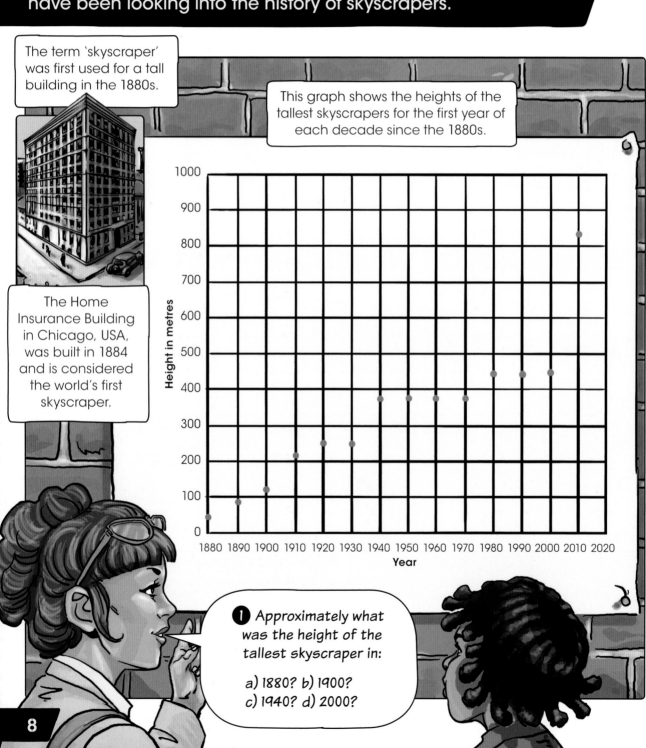

The term 'skyscraper' was first used for a tall building in the 1880s.

The Home Insurance Building in Chicago, USA, was built in 1884 and is considered the world's first skyscraper.

This graph shows the heights of the tallest skyscrapers for the first year of each decade since the 1880s.

Height in metres (y-axis: 0 to 1000)
Year (x-axis: 1880 to 2020)

❶ Approximately what was the height of the tallest skyscraper in:

a) 1880? b) 1900?
c) 1940? d) 2000?

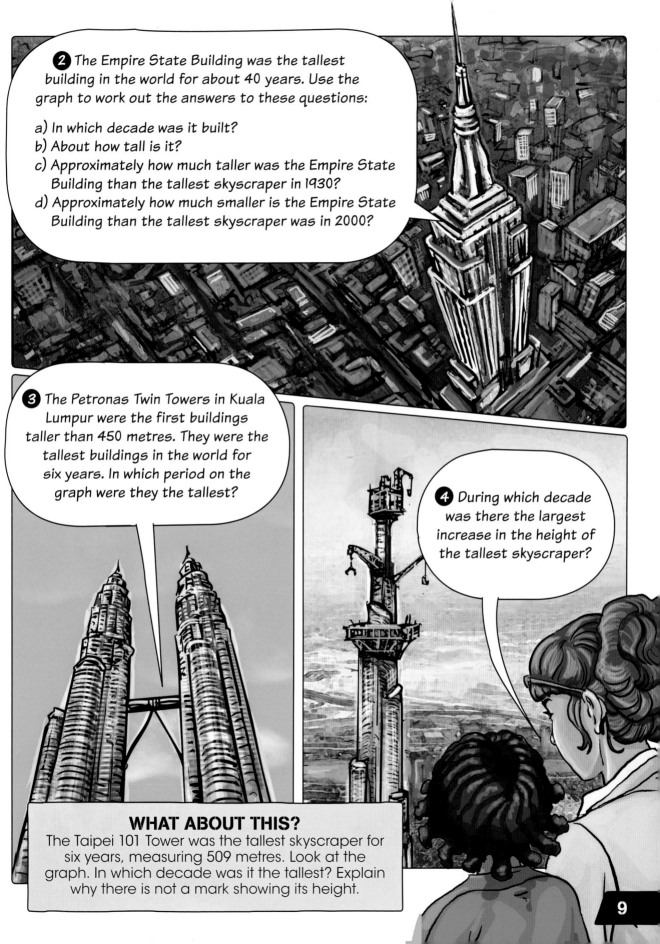

2 The Empire State Building was the tallest building in the world for about 40 years. Use the graph to work out the answers to these questions:

a) In which decade was it built?
b) About how tall is it?
c) Approximately how much taller was the Empire State Building than the tallest skyscraper in 1930?
d) Approximately how much smaller is the Empire State Building than the tallest skyscraper was in 2000?

3 The Petronas Twin Towers in Kuala Lumpur were the first buildings taller than 450 metres. They were the tallest buildings in the world for six years. In which period on the graph were they the tallest?

4 During which decade was there the largest increase in the height of the tallest skyscraper?

WHAT ABOUT THIS?
The Taipei 101 Tower was the tallest skyscraper for six years, measuring 509 metres. Look at the graph. In which decade was it the tallest? Explain why there is not a mark showing its height.

CHOOSING THE SITE

It is important that you choose a good piece of land or site to build your skyscraper on.

You have four sites to choose from and you need to make sure that the one you choose is suitable to build on. Building close to water can mean the foundations have to go deeper, which could be more expensive. Flattening any hills or removing trees may also add problems.

You should also think about the shape of your skyscraper and whether it will fit.

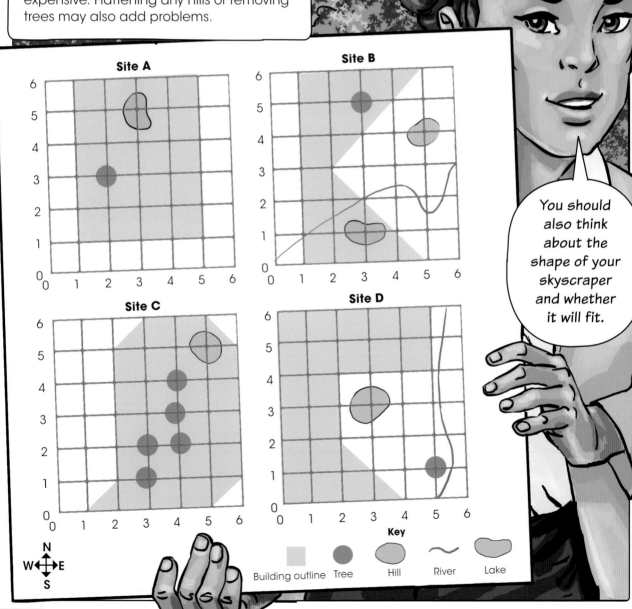

Site A

Site B

Site C

Site D

Key

Building outline   Tree   Hill   River   Lake

N
W E
S

1 On which site would you find:

a) a tree at the position (3, 2)?
b) a lake at (3, 5)?
c) a hill at (5, 5)?
d) the river passing through (6, 3)?

2 What are the co-ordinates of:

a) the tree in site D?
b) the tree in site B?
c) the lake in site A?
d) the hill in site B?

3 Standing at the tree in site B, in which **compass direction** should you walk to reach the lake?

4 Standing at the tree in site D, in which compass direction should you walk to reach the hill?

WHAT ABOUT THIS?
Pick which of the four sites you would choose for your skyscraper. Then work out the **area** of the building's outline by counting squares and half squares.

SECURING THE SITE

Once the site has been cleared, you'll need to fence it off for security and safety reasons before building work can begin.

The fence around the edge of the site is known as the **perimeter** fence.

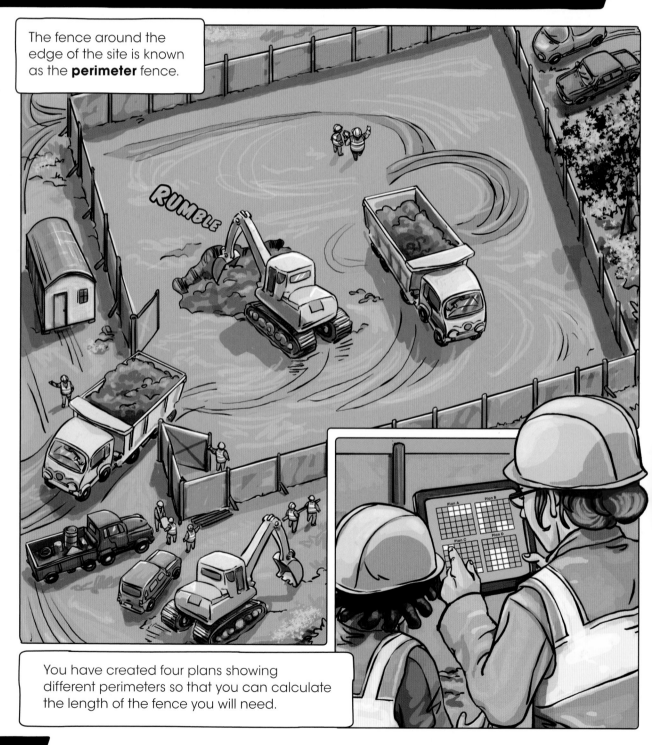

You have created four plans showing different perimeters so that you can calculate the length of the fence you will need.

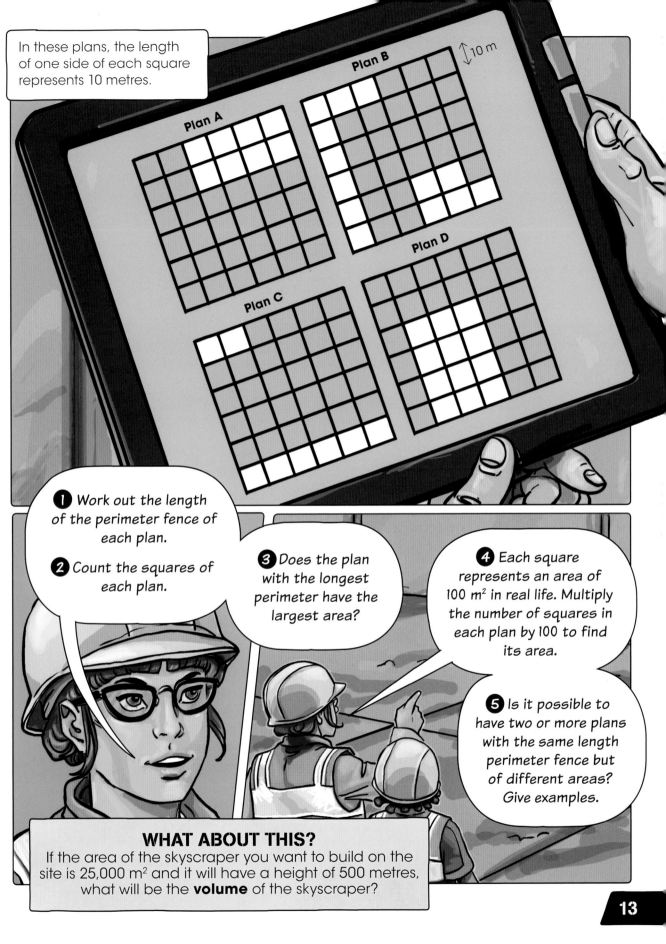

In these plans, the length of one side of each square represents 10 metres.

Plan A

Plan B

Plan C

Plan D

10 m

1 Work out the length of the perimeter fence of each plan.

2 Count the squares of each plan.

3 Does the plan with the longest perimeter have the largest area?

4 Each square represents an area of 100 m² in real life. Multiply the number of squares in each plan by 100 to find its area.

5 Is it possible to have two or more plans with the same length perimeter fence but of different areas? Give examples.

WHAT ABOUT THIS?
If the area of the skyscraper you want to build on the site is 25,000 m² and it will have a height of 500 metres, what will be the **volume** of the skyscraper?

13

DIGGING FOUNDATIONS

Solid foundations are vital if your skyscraper is going to stay up. It is important to dig down until solid ground is reached and put in foundations to support the structure of your building.

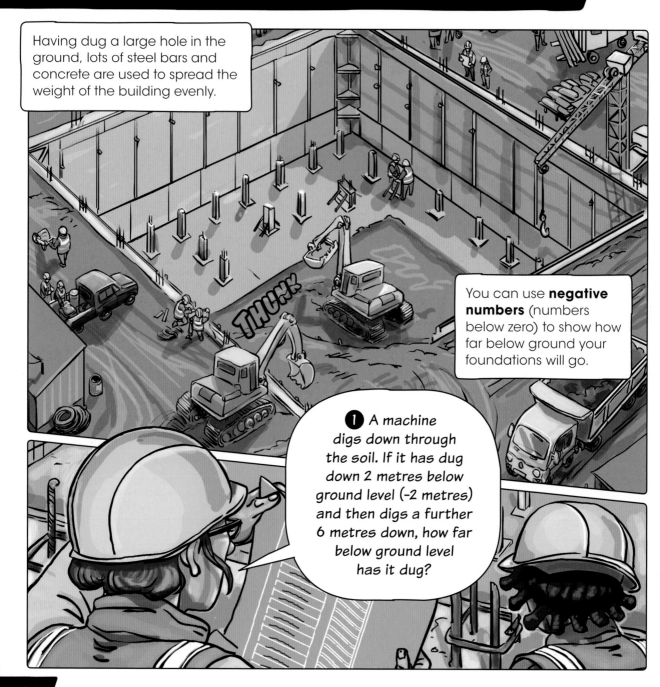

Having dug a large hole in the ground, lots of steel bars and concrete are used to spread the weight of the building evenly.

You can use **negative numbers** (numbers below zero) to show how far below ground your foundations will go.

1 A machine digs down through the soil. If it has dug down 2 metres below ground level (-2 metres) and then digs a further 6 metres down, how far below ground level has it dug?

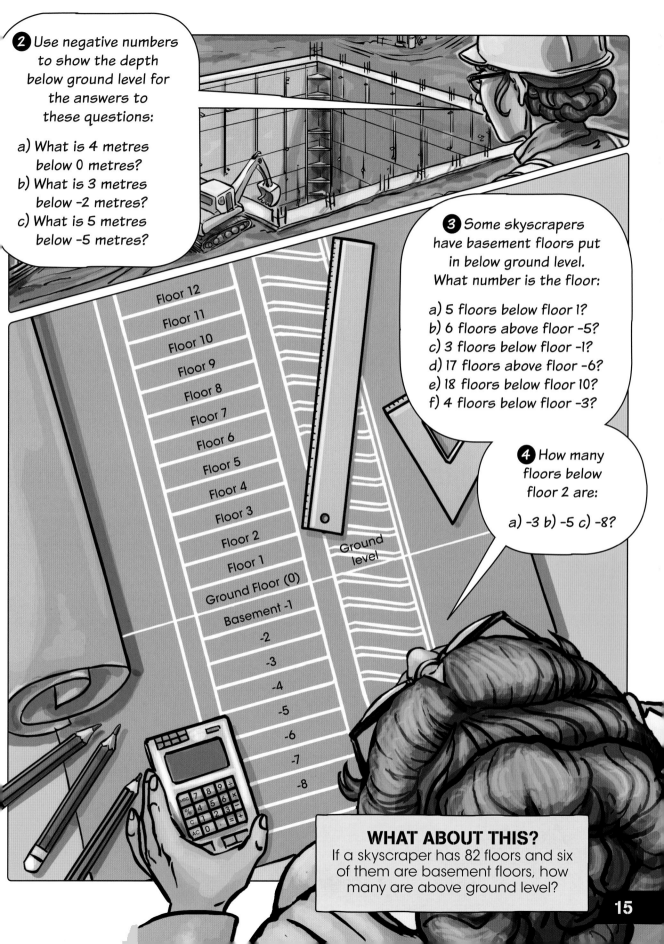

2 Use negative numbers to show the depth below ground level for the answers to these questions:

a) What is 4 metres below 0 metres?
b) What is 3 metres below –2 metres?
c) What is 5 metres below –5 metres?

3 Some skyscrapers have basement floors put in below ground level. What number is the floor:

a) 5 floors below floor 1?
b) 6 floors above floor –5?
c) 3 floors below floor –1?
d) 17 floors above floor –6?
e) 18 floors below floor 10?
f) 4 floors below floor –3?

4 How many floors below floor 2 are:

a) –3 b) –5 c) –8?

Floor 12
Floor 11
Floor 10
Floor 9
Floor 8
Floor 7
Floor 6
Floor 5
Floor 4
Floor 3
Floor 2
Floor 1
Ground Floor (0)
Basement –1
–2
–3
–4
–5
–6
–7
–8

Ground level

WHAT ABOUT THIS?
If a skyscraper has 82 floors and six of them are basement floors, how many are above ground level?

15

STRONG MATERIALS

With strong foundations in place, the main building work on your skyscraper can begin.

Steel girders are needed to make sure the frame of your skyscraper is strong.

Girders are long prisms and usually have a cross-section that looks like the letters I, H or T. These shapes are less likely to bend.

1 The letters I, H and T are all symmetrical, as they have at least one line of **reflective symmetry**. Which of the other capital letters in our alphabet are symmetrical?

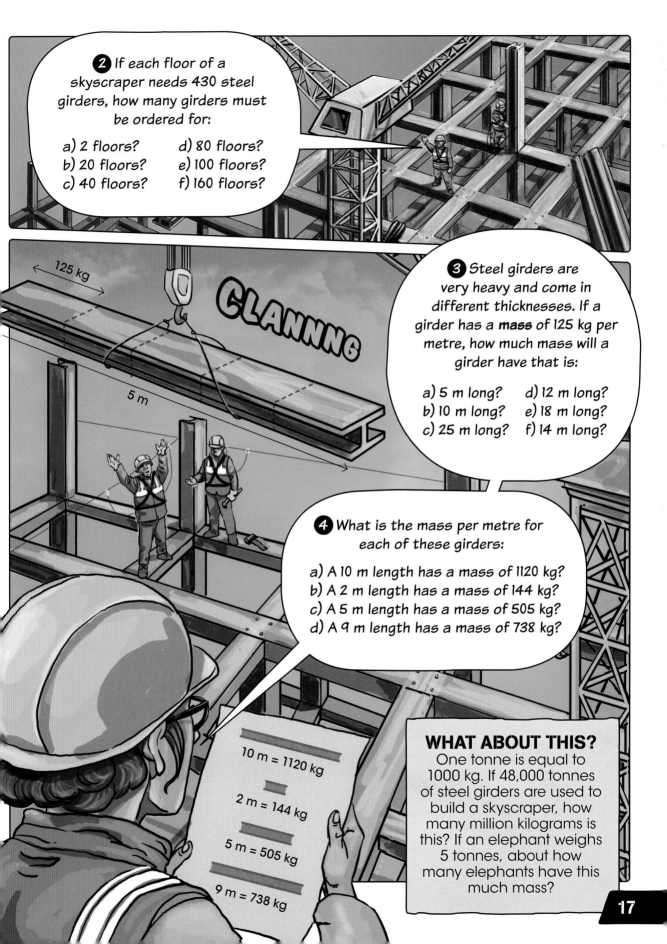

2 If each floor of a skyscraper needs 430 steel girders, how many girders must be ordered for:

a) 2 floors?
b) 20 floors?
c) 40 floors?
d) 80 floors?
e) 100 floors?
f) 160 floors?

125 kg

CLANNNG

5 m

3 Steel girders are very heavy and come in different thicknesses. If a girder has a **mass** of 125 kg per metre, how much mass will a girder have that is:

a) 5 m long?
b) 10 m long?
c) 25 m long?
d) 12 m long?
e) 18 m long?
f) 14 m long?

4 What is the mass per metre for each of these girders:

a) A 10 m length has a mass of 1120 kg?
b) A 2 m length has a mass of 144 kg?
c) A 5 m length has a mass of 505 kg?
d) A 9 m length has a mass of 738 kg?

10 m = 1120 kg

2 m = 144 kg

5 m = 505 kg

9 m = 738 kg

WHAT ABOUT THIS?
One tonne is equal to 1000 kg. If 48,000 tonnes of steel girders are used to build a skyscraper, how many million kilograms is this? If an elephant weighs 5 tonnes, about how many elephants have this much mass?

SKYSCRAPER USES

Skyscrapers are often built to be office blocks, living accommodation, hotels or a mixture of these.

You have been asked to include offices, hotel rooms, flats, restaurants and shops in your skyscraper.

Think about how many floors your skyscraper will have and what fraction or proportion of these floors you will set aside for different uses.

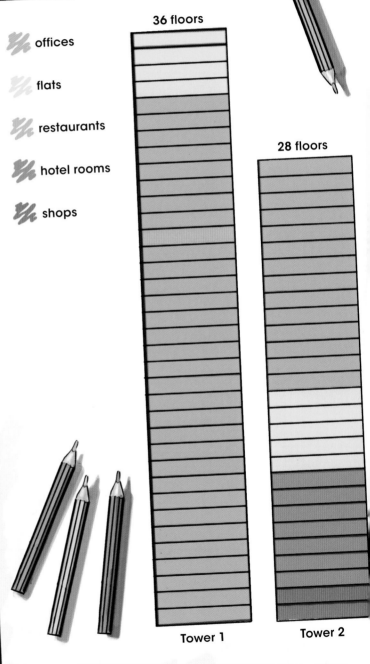

offices

flats

restaurants

hotel rooms

shops

36 floors

28 floors

Tower 1

Tower 2

These pictures are colour-coded to show the floor uses of some skyscrapers.

1 Giving your answer as a **fraction**, write what proportion of:

a) tower 4 is shops
b) tower 1 is restaurants
c) tower 2 is flats
d) tower 3 is restaurants.

2 Giving each answer as a fraction in its simplest form, write what proportion of:

a) tower 2 is shops
b) tower 4 is hotel rooms
c) tower 1 is flats
d) tower 2 is hotel rooms.

3 Work out the proportion of each tower that is offices and **simplify** each fraction if you can.

4 Find out the answer to these questions:

a) Which tower has one quarter of its floors as hotel rooms?
b) Which tower has one eighth of its floors as flats?
c) Which tower has one tenth of its floors as restaurants?

32 floors

30 floors

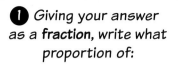

Tower 3   Tower 4

WHAT ABOUT THIS?
"Exactly half of tower ___ is
_____."
Look at the diagrams and find two ways of completing this sentence.

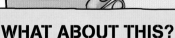

BUILDING YOUR SKYSCRAPER

Your next job is to design the services, such as electrical wiring, telephone connections, heating, plumbing and toilets, for your skyscraper. These go inside the tower and make it a comfortable place to live and work.

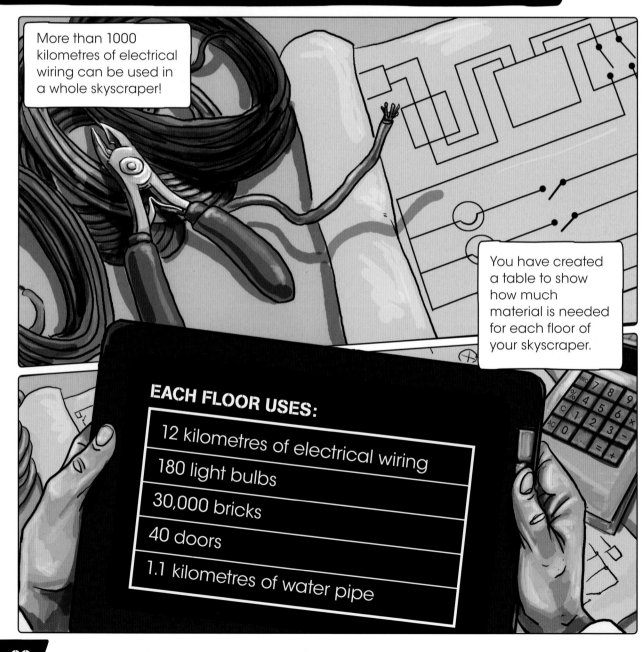

More than 1000 kilometres of electrical wiring can be used in a whole skyscraper!

You have created a table to show how much material is needed for each floor of your skyscraper.

EACH FLOOR USES:

12 kilometres of electrical wiring
180 light bulbs
30,000 bricks
40 doors
1.1 kilometres of water pipe

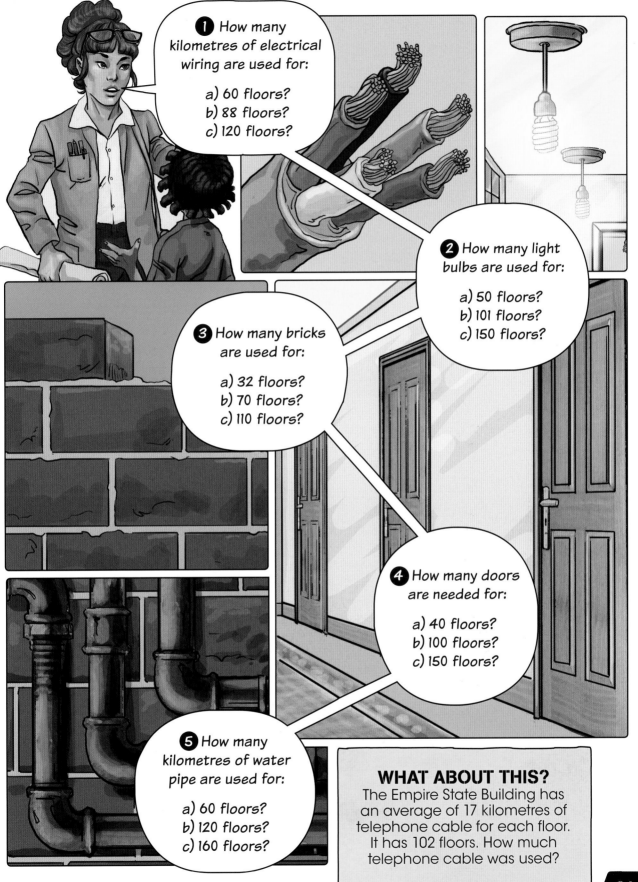

① How many kilometres of electrical wiring are used for:

a) 60 floors?
b) 88 floors?
c) 120 floors?

② How many light bulbs are used for:

a) 50 floors?
b) 101 floors?
c) 150 floors?

③ How many bricks are used for:

a) 32 floors?
b) 70 floors?
c) 110 floors?

④ How many doors are needed for:

a) 40 floors?
b) 100 floors?
c) 150 floors?

⑤ How many kilometres of water pipe are used for:

a) 60 floors?
b) 120 floors?
c) 160 floors?

WHAT ABOUT THIS?
The Empire State Building has an average of 17 kilometres of telephone cable for each floor. It has 102 floors. How much telephone cable was used?

SURVIVING EARTHQUAKES

The latest technology and maths means that skyscrapers can be built taller and stronger than ever before.

Modern materials and building techniques will allow your tower to bend and twist to cope with the most extreme conditions, such as earthquakes and powerful winds.

This table shows the Richter Scale, which measures the seriousness of an earthquake using a scale of 1 (for the weakest) to 12 (for the strongest). The centre of an earthquake is called the epicentre.

1	Usually not felt.
2	Felt only by sensitive people.
3	Vibrations similar to heavy traffic.
4	Rocking of objects.
5	Sleeping people are woken.
6	Damage to buildings within 10s of kilometres from the epicentre.
7	Serious damage up to 100 km from the epicentre.
8	Great destruction, loss of life over several 100 km from the epicentre.
9	Major damage and loss of life over 1000 km from the epicentre.
10	Many buildings are destroyed. There are some landslides.
11	Few buildings remain standing. Bridges and railways are destroyed.
12	Major or complete destruction.

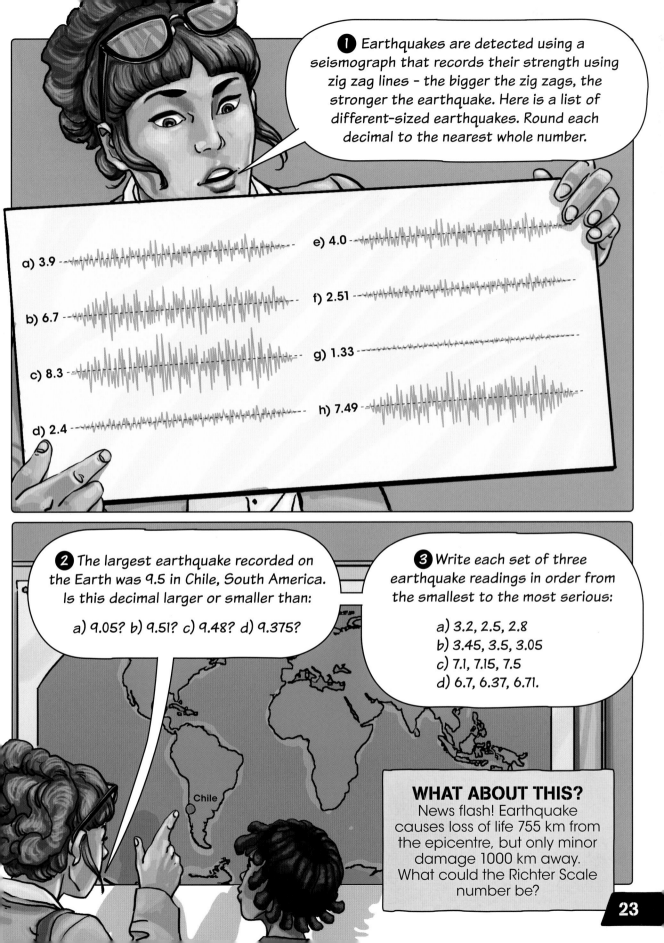

1 Earthquakes are detected using a seismograph that records their strength using zig zag lines - the bigger the zig zags, the stronger the earthquake. Here is a list of different-sized earthquakes. Round each decimal to the nearest whole number.

a) 3.9

b) 6.7

c) 8.3

d) 2.4

e) 4.0

f) 2.51

g) 1.33

h) 7.49

2 The largest earthquake recorded on the Earth was 9.5 in Chile, South America. Is this decimal larger or smaller than:

a) 9.05? b) 9.51? c) 9.48? d) 9.375?

Chile

3 Write each set of three earthquake readings in order from the smallest to the most serious:

a) 3.2, 2.5, 2.8
b) 3.45, 3.5, 3.05
c) 7.1, 7.15, 7.5
d) 6.7, 6.37, 6.71.

WHAT ABOUT THIS?
News flash! Earthquake causes loss of life 755 km from the epicentre, but only minor damage 1000 km away. What could the Richter Scale number be?

EMERGENCY STAIRS

Your skyscraper will need lifts, but it is also important to have staircases for emergencies.

Floor **33**

Floor **31**

Rise height

Tread depth

In a staircase the 'rise height' is the distance from the top of one stair to the top of the next, and the 'tread depth' is the depth of the stair.

The recommended rise height is usually between 16 cm and 22 cm.

1 If the rise height for your staircase is 20 cm, what would be the height of a staircase with each of these numbers of stairs? Give your answers in metres.

a) 10 stairs b) 20 stairs c) 25 stairs.

2 Using your answers to question 1, find out how much shorter each staircase would be if the rise height for each stair was:

a) 18 cm b) 16 cm c) 12 cm.

20 cm

3 m

3 If the distance between the floors of a skyscraper is 3 metres and you put in 15 stairs for each floor, what would the rise height of each stair be?

140
139
138
137

4 A skyscraper has 140 floors, with 15 stairs for each floor. Each stair has a rise height of 19 cm.

a) How many stairs are there altogether?
b) What is the distance between each floor in centimetres?
c) What is the total height of the floors of this skyscraper in metres?

WHAT ABOUT THIS?
Measure the tread depth and rise height of some stairs. Can you work out the total height or total depth of the staircase?

GOING TO THE TOP

It is much faster to travel up and down in a lift than to use the stairs. Some of the largest skyscrapers have more than 100 lifts for all the people moving around.

Your skyscraper will have express lifts that move very quickly, travelling at over 16 metres every second – that is faster than an Olympic sprinter!

WHOOSH

Here are the speeds of the lifts in some of the world's tallest buildings.

NAME	AVERAGE SPEED OF LIFT (METRES PER SECOND)
Empire State Building	6
Jin Mao Building	7
Burj Khalifa	8

Empire State Building

1 The highest a lift will travel in the Empire State building is 318 metres. How many seconds would the lift take to go from ground level to the top, if going at the average speed and not stopping?

2 The highest a lift will travel in the Burj Khalifa building is 504 metres. How many seconds will the lift take to get there?

Burj Khalifa

3 The observation deck of the Jin Mao building is 343 metres up and on the 88th floor.

a) How many seconds would the lift take to reach there from ground level, going at an average speed?
b) If the lift stops four times on its way to the 88th floor and each stop lasts 20 seconds, how long would the journey take? Give your answer in minutes and seconds.

Jin Mao building

4 A lift in a skyscraper took 3 minutes and 34 seconds to travel from ground level to the observation deck.

a) How many seconds is this?
b) If it left ground level at 12:25 and 40 seconds, what time did it reach the observation deck?

WHAT ABOUT THIS?
The Taipei 101 Tower has a lift that can go at about 1008 metres every minute. What is this in metres per second?

KEEPING IT CLEAN

The windows on your skyscraper are all in place
and the towering building itself looks impressive.

How are you going to keep all those
windows clean? You're going to need
some very brave window cleaners!

❶ There are 110 floors on the Willis
Tower in Chicago and each floor has
146 windows. How many windows are
there altogether? Write the answer in
figures and words.

2 The Burj Khalifa tower has 24,000 windows. The area of the glass is 120,000 m². What is the average area of each window?

3 Imagine stepping out to clean windows of the Burj Khalifa tower 800 metres above the ground! What fraction of a kilometre is 800 metres? Give your answer in its simplest form.

4 It takes a team of 36 window cleaners three months to clean the Burj Khalifa tower.

a) How long would you expect it to take 18 window cleaners to do the same job?
b) How many window cleaners might you need to do the same job in 1½ months?
c) How many window cleaners might you need to do the same job in one month?

WHAT ABOUT THIS?
Decide how many floors your skyscraper would have and how many windows for each floor on average. How many windows would this be in total? How long might they take to be cleaned?

ANSWERS

Congratulations! You have built the world's tallest skyscraper! Check your answers here and see how well you did.

PAGES 4–5

1. a) 1 b) 0 c) 8 d) 8 e) 6 f) 0 g) 5

2. a) 2 b) 3 c) 6 d) 6 e) 5 f) 1 g) 5

3. a) cylinder, cone b) cuboid, cylinder, sphere c) square-based pyramid d) cuboid, square-based pyramid e) triangular prism

4. a) 2 b) 7 c) 4 d) 8 e) 4

5. 1 – e, 2 – c and d, 3 – b, 4 – a you wouldn't see 5

PAGES 6–7

1. a) 130 m b) 40 m c) 732 m

2.

NAME	HEIGHT
Big Ben	96 m
The Gherkin	180 m
The Shard	310 m
Empire State Building	381 m
Jin Mao Building	421 m
Petronas Twin Towers	452 m
Taipei 101 Tower	509 m
One World Trade Center	541 m
Makkah Royal Clock Tower	601 m
Shanghai Tower	632 m
Burj Khalifa	828 m

3. a) Shanghai Tower b) One World Trade Center c) The Shard

4.

NAME	HEIGHT TO NEAREST 100M
Big Ben	100 m
The Gherkin	200 m
The Shard	300 m
Empire State Building	400 m
Jin Mao Building	400 m
Petronas Twin Towers	500 m
Taipei 101 Tower	500 m
One World Trade Center	500 m
Makkah Royal Clock Tower	600 m
Shanghai Tower	600 m
Burj Khalifa	800 m

PAGES 8–9

1. a) 40 m b) 120 m c) 380 m d) 450 m

2. a) 1930s b) 380 m c) 130 m d) 70 m

3. 1990–2010

4. 2000–2010

WHAT ABOUT THIS? It was the tallest between 2000–2010. There is no mark because it had been overtaken by the end of the decade.

PAGES 10–11

1. a) Site C b) Site A c) Site C d) Site B

2. a) (5,1) b) (3,5) c) (3,5) d) (5,4)

3. south

4. north west

PAGES 12–13

1. a) 240 m b) 240 m c) 220 m d) 320 m

2. a) 28 squares b) 23 squares
   c) 28 squares d) 24 squares

3. No

4. a) $2800m^2$ b) $2300m^2$ c) $2800m^2$ d) $2400m^2$

5. Yes, A and B have the same perimeters
   but different areas, while A and C have
   the same areas but different perimeters.

WHAT ABOUT THIS? The volume of the
   skyscraper is $12,500,000\ m^3$.

PAGES 14–15

1. 8 m below ground level (-8 m)

2. a) -4 m b) -5 m c) -10 m

3. a) -4 b) 1 c) -4 d) 11 e) -8 f) -7

4. a) 5 b) 7 c) 10

WHAT ABOUT THIS? There are 76 floors
   above ground level.

PAGES 16–17

1. A, B, C, D, E, K, M, O, T, U, V, W, X, Y

2. a) 860 b) 8600 c) 17,200 d) 34,400
   e) 43,000 f) 68,800

3. a) 625 kg b) 1250 kg c) 3125 kg d) 1500 kg
   e) 2250 kg f) 1750 kg

4. a) 112 kg b) 72 kg c) 101 kg d) 82 kg

WHAT ABOUT THIS? It is 48 million kg,
   which is equivalent to 9600 elephants.

PAGES 18–19

1. a) $^1/_{30}$ b) $^1/_{36}$ c) $^5/_{28}$ d) $^3/_{32}$

2. a) $^1/_{14}$ b) $^1/_2$ c) $^1/_9$ d) $^1/_4$

3. 1 – $^{31}/_{36}$, 2 – $^1/_2$, 3 – $^{25}/_{32}$, 4 – $^{11}/_{30}$

4. a) 2 b) 3 c) 4

WHAT ABOUT THIS?
   Exactly half of tower 2 is offices.
   Exactly half of tower 4 is hotel rooms.

PAGES 20–21

1. a) 720 km b) 1056 km c) 1440 km

2. a) 9000 b) 18,180 c) 27,000

3. a) 960,000 b) 2,100,000 c) 3,300,000

4. a) 1600 b) 4000 c) 6000

5. a) 66 km b) 132 km c) 176 km

WHAT ABOUT THIS? 1734 km of telephone cable
   was used.

PAGES 22–23

1. a) 4 b) 7 c) 8 d) 2 e) 4 f) 3 g) 1 h) 7

2. a) larger b) smaller c) larger d) larger

3. a) 2.5, 2.8, 3.2 b) 3.05, 3.45, 3.5
   c) 7.1, 7.15, 7.5 d) 6.37, 6.7, 6.71

WHAT ABOUT THIS? The earthquake
   measured 8 on the Richter Scale.

PAGES 24–25

1. a) 2 m, b) 4 m, c) 5 m

2. a) 20 cm, 40 cm, 50 cm b) 40 cm, 80 cm,
   100 cm c) 80 cm, 160 cm, 200 cm

3. 20 cm

4. a) 2100 b) 285 cm c) 399 m

PAGES 26–27

1. 53 seconds

2. 63 seconds

3. a) 49 seconds b) 2 minutes 9 seconds

4. a) 214 seconds b) 12:29 and 14 seconds

WHAT ABOUT THIS? That is 16.8 metres
   per second.

PAGES 28–29

1. a) 16,060, sixteen thousand and sixty

2. a) $5\ m^2$

3. a) $^4/_5$

4. a) 6 months b) 72 c) 108

GLOSSARY

AREA
The amount of surface a shape covers.

COMPASS DIRECTION
The points found around a compass, including north, south, east and west.

FACE
A surface of a 3D shape.

FRACTION
A part of a whole. The number on the bottom of the fraction (the denominator) tells you how many equal parts the whole has been split into. The number on the top (the numerator) tells you the number of equal parts.

MASS
How much matter there is in an object. Mass is measured using kilograms.

NEGATIVE NUMBERS
These are numbers that are less than zero. They are written using the minus sign.

PERIMETER
The perimeter is the total length around the outside of a shape.

PRISM
A prism is a 3D shape that has the same cross-section throughout its length. For example, a triangular prism has a triangular cross-section.

PYRAMID
A 3D shape that has a polygon base, such as a square or triangle, and triangular sides, which lean inwards and meet at the top in a point.

REFLECTIVE SYMMETRY
A shape or object has reflective symmetry when it has at least one mirror line that can split it into two reflected halves.

ROUND
To round a number to the nearest 10 is to say which multiple of 10 it is closest to. Numbers ending 1 to 4 are rounded down, while numbers ending 5 to 9 are rounded up.

SIMPLIFY
This involves changing a fraction to an equivalent fraction that uses smaller numbers.

VERTICES
Vertices are the corners of a 3D shape. The singular of vertices is vertex.

VOLUME
The volume of a 3D shape is the amount of space it takes up, measured in cubes, such as cubic centimetres (cm^3).

INDEX